It's Christmas Time in the Country

by Judy Condon

Library of Congress Cataloging-in-Publications Data
It's Christmas Time in the Country by Judy Condon
ISBN 978-0-9966965-5-5

Oceanic Graphic Printing, Inc.
105 Main Street
Hackensack, NJ 07601

Printed in China

Layout and Design by Pat Lucas,
    lucasketch_design@yahoo.com
    pat-lucas.fineartamerica.com
Edited by Trent Michaels

Table of Contents

About the Author

Judy Condon is a native New Englander which explains her decorating style and the antiques she collects and sells. Her real passion is 19thC authentic dry red or blue painted pieces. While Judy enjoyed a professional career in education in Connecticut, Judy's weekends were spent at her antique shop, *Marsh Homestead Country Antiques*, located in Litchfield.

Judy accepted an early retirement from education and concentrated her energy and passion for antiques into a fulltime business. Judy maintains a website, *www.marshhomesteadantiques.com* and has been a Power Seller on °eBay for 18 years under the name "superct". Judy has five children and seven grandchildren and enjoys reading, golf, bridge, tennis, and volunteering in the educational system in St Maarten.

After retiring her position as Superintendent of Schools in Connecticut, Judy began writing the "simply country" book series and has completed 44 books to date. The books are now collector items with country decorators who clamor for the inspirational ideas found in the books.

In 2012, Judy met Sherry D Pees, a period home consultant from Ohio and after enthusiastically spirited conversations, decided to co-author *Authenticating a Country Dwelling* which was published in 2013. The book explains by room the difference between country decorating and authenticating a room to replicate one from the 19thC. A sequel, *A Primer for a Country Dwelling*, has been well-received and in a short time has become a 'go to' book for information on authenticating.

In 2014, Judy deviated briefly from the series to write *Nothing Tastes as Good as Skinny*, a tough-love approach and Program for weight loss and weight loss management. In 2014, Judy created the first hand poured 'flameless' battery powered 'country' candle. Since then, thousands of pillars, votives and 6" tapers have been poured and 'grunged' with spices for the country decorator. The candles are sold on °Amazon, her website and on °ebay under the seller ID 'candlelikes'.

Judy's country books are available on her website – *www.marshhomesteadantiques.com*, from °ebay under seller ID 'superct', °Amazon or her email, *marshhomestead@gmail*.com. Ordering is also available through the toll free number 877-381-6682. Judy also maintains a Facebook page 'Marsh Homestead Country Antiques'.

Introduction

It has been a wonderful journey for me during the last 15 years! The strangers who have become friends. The hundreds of homes I've photographed. The tricks I've learned. The decorating hints I've been able to share. During those years, I've gained grandchildren, sent two off to college, become an empty-nester, lost parents, welcomed daughters-in-law and sons-in-law into the family, started a candle business, and . . . moved again!

My friends, I know from your letters, notes of appreciation, phone calls and emails, over the past 15 years, you have experienced some of the same life changing events. I thank you for your support, your interest in my work and most importantly, your friendship.

Those of you who know me well, would acknowledge that sitting around eating bon bons is not in my nature; so while I'm currently working on what may be the last book in the 'simply country' series, I suspect I won't just simply fade into the night! I'm working to publish a children's book I wrote four years ago, *The Adventures of a Coconut Named Burt*, utilizing the talents of six high school students in St. Maarten to illustrate the story.

I love creating, a challenge and taking a risk to start a new adventure. I'm unclear at this point how I will re-invent myself, but I don't think you'll be rid of me quite that easily.

In the meantime, I hope you enjoy *It's Christmas Time in the Country* and continue to draw inspiration from the pictures and ideas homeowners willingly and with love continue to share with us.

Wishing you the merriest of memories from the holiday season and the warmth of all that the holidays offer.

Chapter 1

^ ✿ ^

Mary Amos

So often, part of the charm of our treasured pieces includes their stories: perhaps who we were with, a person or place associated with the pieces, or the details of the hunt. For Mary Amos of Northern Virginia, her collections go well beyond that by creating memories for hundreds of people so that they, too, have a story.

When I first became acquainted with Mary, I was told she was an octogenarian caregiving her 99-year-old mother and that scheduling a photography session in her home might be challenging, let alone completing the follow-up interview. Was I ever wrong!

Mary grew up in Wisconsin, and as a young child watched her mother save her pennies to buy antiques at a second-hand store. Mary caught the bug and 80 years later hasn't lost her love of the patina and colors of original painted pieces, although she admits, "Maybe I have enough."

What I thought was going to be a challenging interview became a bedtime story told by a not-so-elderly woman with an incredible history of giving to others, touching the lives of hundreds, and seizing every opportunity to create memories for everyone in her path. I was mesmerized and moved.

Mary graduated from high school with an art scholarship, but her mother told her that girls might have a hard time as an artist – she should become a teacher or a nurse. Mary elected nursing, and a few years later married an Air Force pilot, which meant constant relocations. The many moves inhibited her chances to become certified as a nurse in each state, so Mary concentrated on making a home for her family of three sons.

Thirty-five years ago Mary was left alone with three sons to parent, and Mary's mother, whom she describes as her best friend, moved in to help.

Unable to fulfill her dream to live in an older house, Mary and her mother were determined to age a newer home to perfection. Together they renovated Mary's home, oftentimes without help. They ripped up wall-to-wall carpeting in 3' wide strips and hauled it to the curb; they gathered old boards which they carefully sanded and restored to be used as flooring when they amassed enough to cover a room. Mary seized the opportunity to accept salvaged materials such as early pavers, and painstakingly removed cement from them by sanding to repurpose the pavers for lintels and flooring.

Mary and her mother began to attend flea markets as early as the doors opened – sometimes 4 AM so as not to miss anything. They left the markets each week with their treasures hanging from their trunk and car windows.

As they filled each room, Mary and her mother realized they were creating a little museum of American life and decided to open their doors to schools, teaching students from elementary age to college students about life in America 'back then'.

The working early 19thC tall clock in the front hallway features wooden gears with weights – small tin pails filled with pebbles.

For example, she used the butter churn with its dasher to demonstrate how butter was made and fascinated students with the finished product using her butter press collection with its variety of imprints to make patterned butter pats. Using her antique candlemolds, Mary and her mother showed the students how dipping the wick up and down numerous times into hot wax would accumulate wax on the wick until at last a candle was formed. They used bayberry scent and related to students the popularity of its fragrance to the settlers on the east coast where pine trees were prevalent.

In winter, Mary's mother served homemade cookies with hot chocolate for the students; in summer cookies were offered with lemonade. Mary and her mother created enough lifelong memories that even today they occasionally enjoy the large collection of thank-you notes they've received over the years. The day before I spoke with Mary, a man in his mid-40s had just visited – a man she met over 20 years ago – who asked for Mary's help in finding the period pieces like those Mary collected. I asked Mary if she and her mother still talked about those experiences; not only do they reminisce, but just that afternoon over a lunch of 'high protein casserole', they recalled some of the children they had met and occasionally still heard from.

I thought that Mary's role as caregiver to her mother must be difficult at her age – all the while holding a full-time job –

Mary covered all the lampshades in the house with vintage homespun, and chose salt-glazed stoneware as lamp bases.

The folk art barn in the corner of the room is one of three Mary owns; the Brown Swiss cows speak to Mary's heritage.

wrong again! In addition, Mary offers her time to a local charity. She related that 10 years ago, a young woman at her church wished to give all her wedding presents to someone needing help. From that act of kindness, a group called 'Gracing Spaces' was formed. Using a social worker in the area who identifies families in need, Mary and nine other women meet every Wednesday in the basement of the church to gather, repair, and distribute to needy families bedding, furniture, and other necessities – sometimes outfitting as many as 10 homes in any given week. Mary said she often resembles a bag lady going around in search of donations. Those donations often require attention and Mary spends her time at home laundering and mending bedding and towels, refinishing furniture, or reframing pictures. I commented that she certainly keeps busy and she responded, "Well, it certainly keeps me young."

The early high chair in the dining room evokes a memory for Mary as it was used by one of her sons since he was old enough to sit up. In the chair now sits a vintage Amish doll. Since the Amish don't believe in creating anything in the image of God, they omit putting a face on their dolls.

Mary changed the original purpose of some of the rooms to create a dining room large enough to accommodate a farm table that seats her family of eleven. The 19thC table features a two-board top in untouched condition. The rare matched set of eight chairs retains their original blue paint.

Mary built the mantel herself using salvaged wood from the firehouse in Old Town Alexandria. The shelf holds an exquisite collection of 18thC pewter. Mary didn't care for the color of the bricks and carefully aged them with paint.

Both 19thC stepbacks in blue paint are filled with stacks of colorful original painted pantry boxes of various sizes. Mary displays a gorgeous stack of graduated mustard and red painted firkins alongside. After almost 50 years, Mary can't always remember where she found the boxes or the circumstances around the find but she still appreciates with awe the magnificent surface and color of each.

Ten years ago, Mary built an addition which created an open and bright sitting room. The hired man's bed beneath the window dates to the mid-19thC, while the dry sink with its unique size is filled with painted bowls and boxes.

Did I mention that Mary is a self-taught artist and has won a number of awards at juried shows?

Mary painted the back of each tread in what she calls the 'story of us': a picture of a dog (she rescues dogs), willow trees symbolizing immortality, and a church scene showing the date of one son's marriage. Mary confessed she's not finished yet and just has to find the time to add other details, such as recognition of the marriages of her other sons.

The 19thC hanging cupboard in the upstairs hallway is filled with Mary's sewing supplies including over 100 spools of thread.

Mary shared that growing up in rural Wisconsin and living on Air Force bases, sometimes resources were scarce, so out of necessity she taught herself to sew all her own clothes and, even as a college student, designed and made dresses for her classmates' special occasions.

Upstairs, each bed is draped with a vintage quilt. Mary's mother quilts and is an accomplished weaver of coverlets, which Mary stores safely in a linen cupboard. The little sawbuck table is one of three Mary owns – purchased many years ago at flea markets and shows such as The York Antique Show in York, Pennsylvania. The blocks on the table spell the name of one of Mary's grandsons who sleeps in the room.

Mary made the shutters throughout the house, deliberately leaving 1/4" between boards to represent natural shrinkage that would have occurred over the past 100 years.

Mary's home was first photographed at the end of the fall season. Mary invited us to return after she decorated three unique early feather trees that enables Mary's chapter to introduce us to the holiday season.

Interestingly, Mary's collection of Byer's Choice carolers includes only vendors. The miniature nutcrackers in the basket are each signed 'Steinbeck'.

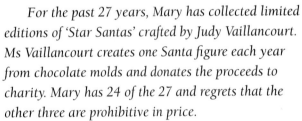

For the past 27 years, Mary has collected limited editions of 'Star Santas' crafted by Judy Vaillancourt. Ms Vaillancourt creates one Santa figure each year from chocolate molds and donates the proceeds to charity. Mary has 24 of the 27 and regrets that the other three are prohibitive in price.

The top shelf of the 19thC bucket bench, seen on page 14, holds a collection of carved angel figures.

The feather tree seen above measures almost 7' tall and is decorated with vintage hand-blown ornaments and cotton birds. The crafted village houses below date as well to the early 20thC.

The 5' tall feather tree right is displayed on a stand with a vintage twig fence surround. The tree holds early ornaments and retains the original candleholders on the branches.

Each tin house in the village is intricately crafted; remnants of vintage cellophane can even be seen in their windows.

The reindeer on the mantel were made by Barbara Stein. The tree at the left side of the mantel is fashioned with bark. The Santa figures on the right are early candy containers.

The tree in the early painted mustard bucket is filled with cotton ornaments that predate glass ornaments. Mary's research shows that each fruit is associated with a legend. The apple is the traditional Christian symbol of temptation, while the star display made from an apple slice brings good health and fortune in the coming year. Oranges, scarce during winter months, were treasured and left in the stockings of good girls and boys. Oranges were among the first glass ornaments made. Plums have been associated with the holidays since the 17thC when the famous English dessert, plum pudding, gained popularity. A carrot was a traditional gift to a bride, believed to bring her good luck in the kitchen. Birds were often thought of as the universal symbol of happiness and joy – considered by many to be necessary on all trees.

Mary never sits still. When not working at the church or taking care of her mother, she works with homeowners as an interior designer! Mary is listed on Angie's List and presently works with three clients decorating their homes, teaching them in much the same manner as she taught young children years ago.

Mary's philosophy is that a well-balanced life makes use of every minute and fills your time with what makes you happy. She likened her approach to a butterfly that flits around to light on numerous spots – in her case, the many people she has encountered and who touched her life. I marveled at all those connections, to which she humbly replied, "I was adopted by a young woman in Houston many years ago who was in labor and alone. I accompanied her to the hospital and helped with her newborn for two years. She tells me every time she sees a butterfly, she thinks of me."

When I hung up, I sat for a few minutes pondering all that Mary had shared and admitted that I, too, would think of Mary each time I saw a butterfly, and she could add me to her long list of those she has touched.

Chapter 2

Jim and Linda Babb

There are homemakers and there are homemakers! Linda Babb of Johnson City, Tennessee exemplifies 'making a home' as she loves change and thinks nothing of changing rooms on a regular basis – even changing houses! Her husband Jim, who Linda refers to as 'Gem', thinks nothing of the changes and supports Linda 100%. As Linda said, "If the queen ain't happy . . . the king ain't happy!" While changing colors or shifting furniture is a common occurrence with us country homemakers, few of us have bought and sold seven houses over the course of our marriage . . . even selling and buying back one favorite along the way.

Jim was stationed in Germany in 1969 in the Air Force as was Linda's stepfather. Linda and Jim met there and married two years later, moving to Tennessee where Jim was employed as an administrator with the Veterans Outpatient Department. Linda, originally from Florida, had always liked country décor and gradually

shifted from cute ducks with hats to colonial country. In 1987, Linda opened a shop in the basement called Country at Heart. It was so successful that she opened a storefront that she operated until 1993 when she decided to sell the business and focus her energies on decorating.

Many of the moves were as a result of wanting a bigger house, or a smaller house, or simply because Linda yearned for a fresh pallet. During the last move, a downsize, Linda decided to keep only high-quality pieces. She prefers darker red and brown wash tones rather than mixing a variety of early painted pieces.

Jim selected the trim color – 'Colonial Beige' by Valspar. Linda's basket collection is one of her favorites, and the broad 19thC cupboard in the Sitting Room is ideal for display. Jim and Linda extensively remodeled the house including crown molding in each room. The banister back chair was crafted by Roger Mason of Old Virginia Trading Company.

Linda loves to sew and made the window treatments throughout the house as well as decorative pillows.

During the holidays, Linda decorates with simple greens and assorted fruits such as pomegranates, pineapples, pears, and oranges; their aroma fills the house.

The early pie safe with red wash pictured below is Linda's favorite piece; it was found in Virginia's Shenandoah Valley.

Linda is partial to early horses and owns five. One stands on top of the pie safe in front of a vintage 'hit or miss' hooked rug.

The house originally featured a column on either side of the opening between the living and dining rooms. Jim and Linda removed the columns which didn't fit the décor and Linda now divides the room using comfortable armchairs where they can enjoy their morning coffee. The hutch table dates to the mid 19thC.

The corner of the dining room holds a tall feather tree which Linda made! This is a great idea and once she shared her process, I couldn't wait to try one myself.

Linda purchased an inexpensive artificial tree and then thinned the branches with wire cutters to give the tree the sparse appearance of a feather tree. With more than one blister on her hands, she then cut each of the needles to approximately a quarter to half an inch. Despite the blisters and the mess, she's thrilled with the end result.

An early trencher holds three large pomegranates, greenery, and an old leather Bible.

The large walnut stepback is filled with two other favorite collections – early pewter and leather bound books.

Linda added an early mantel at one end of the room to offer a more balanced feel. The mantel provides an ideal decorating option.

Linda made the hanging candles by using store-bought candles that she whittled down to expose the wicks. She then aged the surface with beeswax and wrapped the wick around an iron rod.

Linda found the hanging red wash cupboard, dating to the mid 1800s, at the Seville Antique Center in Seville, Ohio. The pie safe below holds early leather bound books.

The center of the table holds a vintage box filled with early stone fruit.

The 12' living room ceilings dwarf the original fireplace. Jim and Linda had a contractor rebuild the fireplace and extend it upward with a cupboard to house a television.

Linda found the small tavern table at a local antique shop.

The large schoolmasters' desk fills the corner and holds many leather bound books, as well as an original feather quill pen and old Bible. The sampler on the wall is 19thC.

Linda made all the bed linens and curtains in the master bedroom. She used Lindsey-Woolsey fabric purchased at The Seraph to create the bed curtains.

Linda dressed a tin sconce over the headboard with a bit of greenery. The portrait in the corner is an antique. A small vintage box below holds stone fruit.

The 19thC highboy retains its original vinegar painted surface. On top stands an old green onion bottle. A small Chippendale mirror hangs above. Linda purchased the pair of make-do chairs at Angel House in Brookfield, Massachusetts.

A rice-carved bed in the guest room is draped with a Lindsey-Woolsey coverlet from The Seraph.

A tin candelabra stands on a 19thC small tavern table. The Chippendale mirror, part of another favorite collection, hangs above.

Linda feels sure that this house is their last move but continues to tweak rooms. She was in the process of converting two guestrooms to a small sitting room where she could sew, and the other a comfortable den that Jim could enjoy.

Linda makes school girl samplers which she sells on ⁰eBay under the name 'theprimitivestitcher'. She also maintains a site at *www.picturetrail.com/theprimitivestitcher*.

Chapter 3

Matt and Jody Ellenwood

"Don't throw it away" is Jody Ellenwood's hue and cry! Some of Jody's favorite pieces are those treasures she intends to have her husband Matt 'recreate'! You'll notice them mingled around their 1940s ranch-style home in Fort Wayne, Indiana.

Jody and Matt love working together on projects; Jody has the vision and Matt the talent to bring Jody's ideas to life. Jody marvels that Matt never complains about his ongoing 'honey do' list!

Matt and Jody have been remodeling since they bought their house 20 years ago. Jody can't really say they have been updating; in essence they age each room – oftentimes with old barn boards salvaged from a nearby 1800s barn. Although Matt travels over an hour each way to work as a supervisor with Keystone RV, he is always eager to tackle another project.

Jody attributes her attraction to country décor to a small holiday tree she places on the vanity in her master bathroom each holiday season. Ten Christmases ago, Jody walked into a shop named Thankful Heart in Shipshewana, Indiana and fell in love! She's gone back often and surmises she and Matt are one of the shop's best customers.

At the time, Jody and Matt were facing an empty nest which Jody confesses made the house entirely too quiet. To soothe her heartache, Jody poured herself into redecorating room by room while gathering country accents wherever she traveled. Matt was 100% supportive but had one request: comfort. Jody compromised with leather furniture in the Great Room which she accents with early pieces such as the trunk used as a coffee table. On top rests an early repurposed box and handcrafted fabric reindeer.

Jody loves the affordability of early barrels to create a display surface and enhance the primitive effect. Arnett's Santa figures can be seen on top of a barrel and an upended toolbox.

Matt made the wall Nativity above the reindeer crafted from early grain sacks.

Jody purchased the artificial tree at Thankful Heart. Brown-papered packages add to the vignette.

A smaller Vienna tree stands at the other side of the couch.

Jody and Matt hope to replace some of their larger pieces with antiques, but in the meantime Jody has developed a process for aging new pieces. When she and Matt purchased the large stepback at Thankful Heart, it was painted a bright, garish yellow. Jody applied Valspar 'Antique Glaze' from Lowes using a cloth.

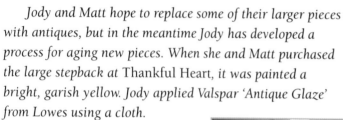

Matt and Jody recently added a slate hearth to the fireplace and a surround that Matt crafted using salvaged barn wood. Jody repainted the bricks which were previously an unsightly pink.

The kitchen cabinets are maple and Amish-made; the counters are Corean. Jody receives many questions through Facebook about her curtains over the sink. She boiled black walnuts from her yard to create a dye, then stained two packages of cheesecloth she bought for $4.

Matt built the laundry area with old wood and square nails.

Matt also built the buttery at the end of the kitchen which affords Jody an excuse and opportunity to hunt for smaller treasures. She plans to gradually upgrade all the pieces to early treen.

The pie safe was built with old wood and 'rat wire' which features larger holes than window screen and smaller than chicken wire. Matt distressed the wire with muriatic acid.

Using barn wood, Matt built the box in front of the window to conceal a trash basket.

The walls in the master bedroom are painted with Sherwin-Williams 'Cardboard'. The coverlet on the bed is from Family Heirloom Weavers.

Jody used a stitched runner that she wrapped around a small pillow. Jody doesn't own a sewing machine and hand-stitched all the pillow shams.

Jody enjoys using fresh greens from the single pine tree on their property. She supplements the aroma of fresh pine by burning a candle scented with maple syrup.

Matt and Jody purchased an old general store counter at Thankful Heart. Matt worked his magic and repurposed it into the vanity in the master bathroom. The holiday tree on top is the same tree mentioned at the beginning of the chapter that Jody fell in love with 10 years ago.

Jody used two shower panels with the popular 'Lover's Knot' pattern to make their shower curtain. A second rod on the tub side of the curtain holds a plastic liner.

Future projects include the addition of a front porch, adding barn wood beams to the ceiling, and crafting a vanity from an old whiskey barrel.

Jody enjoys the blog she created on Facebook titled *Primitive Home Decorating*. Through it she has met many new friends and has over 6,000 followers who share their homes and ideas. While Jody thoroughly enjoys the friends and joy of sharing, she most appreciates the inner peace her home provides. The sign over their mantel seems to say it all. 'It is well with my soul'.

Chapter 4

❧ ✿ ☙

Jeff and Greta Dycus

Despite the fact that Jeff and Greta Dycus lived in a beautiful farmhouse surrounded by rolling hills and meadows, Jeff telephoned Greta at work one day two years ago and said, "You're not going to believe what house is for sale." They made an offer the next day on the house they had eyed for years!

The house, located in Sharpe, Kentucky, dates to 1904 and was built by a doctor who successfully operated a working farm, which explains the numerous outbuildings on their two acres – two barns, a shed, and a smokehouse that Greta admits still smells like ham.

Jeff and Greta both grew up in nearby Paducah, and although neither grew up surrounded by country décor, they enjoy not only the hunt for unique pieces but tend to gravitate toward treasures that

might require a bit of 'tweaking'. Jeff, a chemical engineer at a plastics company, doesn't hesitate to repurpose a find or build it from scratch. Greta feels the same way and when not at the local middle school where she works as a guidance counselor assistant, she dreams of how to make something out of nothing, as she calls it.

When Jeff and Greta moved in two years ago, the house needed little work as the previous two owners were antique collectors and shared the same style of decorating as Greta.

Greta uses a variety of Facebook groups such as Log Cabin Primitives *to sell drieds and her other creations, similar to those pictured left on the table in the front entrance. The treen bowl is filled with wax fruit purchased at Olde Glory in Waynesville, Ohio, and from* Arnett's Country Store.

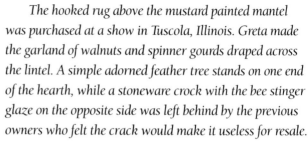

The hooked rug above the mustard painted mantel was purchased at a show in Tuscola, Illinois. Greta made the garland of walnuts and spinner gourds draped across the lintel. A simple adorned feather tree stands on one end of the hearth, while a stoneware crock with the bee stinger glaze on the opposite side was left behind by the previous owners who felt the crack would make it useless for resale.

The large cupboard in original green paint is a built-in that Greta uses to store her large collection of early coverlets.

Jeff and Greta found the make-do dry sink at Twin Lakes Antique Mall. The large punched tin lamp was bought off the back of a truck at The Burlington Antique Market in Burlington, Kentucky. A folk art Santa, fashioned with an old quilt, was purchased at a yard sale for $5!

Greta decorates the soft white tree with a single strand of battery-powered yellow lights which cast a lovely color on what Greta thinks was the top of a much larger tree.

Jeff and Greta made the make-do chair from a $5 auction find; Jeff rebuilt the frame and Greta upholstered it.

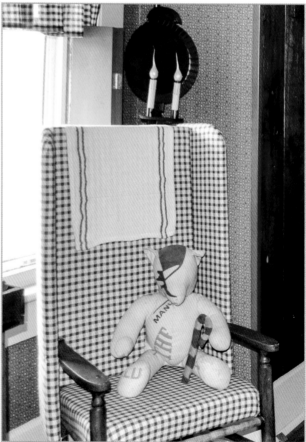

The farm table in the dining room was made by a local craftsman. It is one piece which Jeff and Greta hope to replace with a larger antique table when they find one.

Greta was drawn to the mid-19thC jelly cupboard because it features an old spoon holder. Greta uses the top to hold treen doughbowls. Draped on the door is a vintage remnant of a blue calico quilt. The shelf above displays mortar and pestles.

Betty Alexander, whose home was featured in an earlier book, made the Santa figure on the table.

Jeff built the large stepback and designed it to accommodate Greta's collection of Sturbridge Village redware as well as some of the many pantry boxes in Greta's collection. Greta painted and distressed the cupboard using a deep red paint and dark Briwax.

The pie safe pictured above belonged to Jeff's mother; it needed some restoration and two new doors. Jeff painstakingly punched the tin panels and rebuilt the cabinet. He used an old tin funnel and pie plate to create the lamp on top. Greta stitched the two samplers on the left while Jeff made the frames.

Greta opted to keep the kitchen cupboards red which were original to the house. She and Jeff refinished the pine counters, and after sanding, applied numerous coats of dark stain and varnish.

Greta dressed up the chimney across from the kitchen sink by adding a mantel that Jeff crafted and then staged a fireplace. The mid-19thC hanging cupboard to the left is the oldest piece that Jeff and Greta own.

Jeff and Greta purchased the mustard pie safe at an estate auction of a woman who turned out to be Greta's 7th grade teacher.

Greta knew when she purchased a pair of original painted doors at auction for $3 that she would find a use for them. Jeff used them to create a small buttery, shown above, in the back entrance off the kitchen. He also made the two small hornbeams on the shelf from logs he gathered from their previous property.

Greta uses one wall of the screened porch at the back of the house to display a collection of brooms, tools, and lanterns. Some of her drieds are also pictured.

Greta painted the old bed they found at a yard sale. The cover is an early blanket with many old repairs, which to Greta's eye only serves to add charm. The throw at the foot of the bed is from Family Heirloom Weavers.

The green chest at the end of the bed was purchased at Gathering on the Priairie in Arthur, Illinois. The tool caddy belonged to the previous owner and was purchased by Jeff and Greta at the estate auction. The penny quilt was a left behind treasure. One of the barns on the property served as an antique shop operated by the previous two homeowners. For the time being, Jeff and Greta use it as a getaway spot, although Greta dreams of one day reopening a shop in the space.

Jeff made the quilt rack where Greta displays old quilts including some family pieces.

Greta decorates the large live tree with only small lights and raffia. The old box alongside was found in their other barn.

The barn siding dates to the early 1900s.

The cupboard seen left was repurposed into a dry sink and now displays a number of painted bowls.

Jeff and Greta worked their magic on the cabinet below and converted a bright blue cupboard with pink hearts into a piece more fitting for the barn. A large hole in the back is covered with an early cutting board.

Jeff brought out his hammer and nails one more time to create the punched tin panels on the pie safe seen below that was found in Florence, Kentucky. The large gourd on top was a 'throw away' as it is cracked in the back. Greta placed a brick inside the gourd to stabilize it and who would guess!

With three grown children and pre-grandchildren, Jeff and Greta are, "Living the life with lots of time to play". Greta confessed, "We do what we can with the pieces we find" . . . offering credibility to the old adage, 'One man's trash is another man's treasure'.

Chapter 5

Harry and Debbie Shields

During the holiday season, we are absorbed in sharing and giving to our family members and friends. We bustle about preparing our homes and hearts for a season of celebration. Ten years ago, Harry and Debbie Shields of Hubbard, Ohio reached beyond their family and friends and gave of themselves to create a holiday memorial which is still enjoyed and revered today.

Harry and Debbie both enjoy landscaping and gardening, and those interests led to their restoring a city park. They raised funds and volunteered their labor and time to landscape the park and remodel a small cottage in the park. They turned the interior of the cottage into Santa's living room and brought Santa to visit area children for a week every December. Debbie has always has a fondness for Santa and has been collecting Santa's for most of her adult life. In 2015 they turned the maintenance of the park and Santa's visit over to the town, allowing Harry to recover from brain surgery and enjoy some free time to pursue his other hobbies. They still love to reminisce about the children that visit, their excitement, their nervousness, the looks of awe at seeing Santa, and their happiness and joy and little voices exclaiming 'Santa said he's going to bring me what I want because I told him I've been good!'

Harry works as a CNC machinist while Debbie is a homemaker, but previously she participated in country shows under the name *Shield's Tavern Antiques*. During the 80s, Debbie was invited by her

sister to attend an antique fair, despite the fact that she had no interest in antiques; she only agreed to go to spend time with her sibling. Debbie ended up buying so much that she recalls sitting in the back seat of her sister's car buried under treasures piled high on her lap and hanging out the windows. Thirty years ago, Harry and Debbie purchased their 1930s home and began to work toward creating a country-decorated haven.

The exterior paint is 'Fairview Taupe' by Benjamin Moore.

Debbie enjoys collecting stoneware salt-glazed crocks and displays almost 60 of them throughout the house. An Arnett's Santa figure nestles behind an ovoid jug on the mantel. Debbie purchased the 19thC portrait at the Zoar Harvest Festival in Zoar, Ohio a number of years ago; it exhibits no provenance, but Debbie was drawn to the sitter's kind face.

The drop leaf table to the left of the fireplace is a perfect fit and the price was even better. Debbie found it a few houses down the street sitting at the curb for garbage pick-up; needless to say, she didn't hesitate!

Harry and Debbie enjoy traveling and often visit New England for antiques. In the early 1990s they discovered The Brimfield Antique Show in Massachusetts and purchased the large pie safe to the right of the fireplace. A large Arnett's Santa stands on top beside a folk art crafted horse purchased from a Facebook friend in Medina, Ohio.

The flame stitch fireside chair was purchased from Trudy Nelson, a dealer from Petersburg, Ohio but designed by The Seraph.

Debbie repurposed a primitive plate rack made by Cabin Creek 1850 owner Heather Shreves and uses it as a cage to hold a reindeer and Santa.

Harry and Debbie bought both the red painted chest and the large cupboard beside the fireside chair at auction. The color of the cupboard blends beautifully with the tones of the chair's fabric.

Debbie has such a large collection of Santa figures and vintage Christmas memorabilia that she selects a different sampling each year to decorate.

The chest that serves as a coffee table is full of wonderful early holiday pieces, from miniature Santas to a small reindeer-drawn sleigh – a gift from a friend many years ago.

Tucked behind the sofa, a basket holds a variety of Santa figures dating to the 1940s. Debbie limits the Santas she displays as her young niece finds some of their facial expressions frightening.

Beneath the tree at the base of the stairs is a toy truck that once belonged to Harry's father.

Harry and Debbie purchased the Hancock Shaker ladderback chair at a shop in Maine. The top of the desk holds a wig stand purchased at a show in Ohio, a beaver hat, leather books, and pair of old spectacles.

The dining room table was custom build by J.L. Treharn; the Windsor chairs are from DR Dimes. The child's glider rocking horse was found at an auction in Pennsylvania.

Harry and Debbie hope to replace the early pie safe someday, but in the meantime enjoy its original surface and aged rusted screen doors.

Harry and Debbie removed the glass doors from the built-in corner cupboard and covered the varnished wood with a coat of dark red paint.

Debbie purchased the cake crock on the top shelf from a neighborhood friend who owned an antique shop. The friend gave the shop's bell on the shelf next to the basket of elves to Debbie as a remembrance after the shop closed; her friend has since passed away. The iron Punch and Judy bank holds special meaning to Harry as it belonged to his great-grandfather.

Debbie decorates the early tin candlebox seasonally and feels it shows better on the wall than the mantel.

The table is set with paper thin glass goblets from Harry's grandmother and a set of Friendly Village dinnerware that once belonged to Harry's grandmother. Debbie once owned a set of Corelle dinnerware and confessed to his grandmother one day that she hated it; his grandmother admitted that she didn't like her Friendly Village set. They swapped and each felt like the winner.

The large cupboard is filled with pewter, early redware, and stoneware crocks. Debbie mingles Santa figures and greenery to add a festive flair.

The pocket watch belonged to Debbie's grandfather. It rests beside one of many Indian arrowheads found on Harry's family farm and an old tintype photograph of one of Harry's ancestors.

Debbie managed to find the perfect spot for a small farm worktable where she placed a postal sorting rack. Debbie found the early soldier's books at a shop in Adamstown, Pennsylvania.

Debbie's great-grandmother was a self-taught artist; she rendered the oil painting on the wall that depicts waterfalls and pools where she gathered water and did the laundry as a child in the Hudson Valley of New York.

Debbie debated long and hard before plunging in and painting the kitchen cabinetry with a Sherwin-Williams selection called 'Dapper Tan'. She is thrilled with the result and pleased that the lighter color has brightened the kitchen. The paint tone contrasts nicely with the laminate charcoal black countertops.

I love the age and look of the cutting board with rounded corners to the left of the sink.

Debbie was at an auction when she mentioned to a dealer that she was looking for a butcher block table. He was kind enough to refer her to the owner of a butcher shop he knew was selling one. Debbie was thrilled when she met the owner and he only wanted $30 for the piece. The color fits perfectly and provides another surface for Debbie's Santa figures and treen bowls.

The table in the breakfast area is an old worktable with original red paint. The table had a linoleum top which Harry and Debbie removed to expose the original wood. What an ideal spot for a quiet cup of coffee.

Despite the faux fireplace, the breakfast nook at one end of the kitchen is warm and cozy.

Harry made a lid for the 15-gallon stoneware crock that serves as a trash receptacle alongside the dry sink.

A Family Heirloom Weaver's *coverlet is used on the custom-made bed by J.L. Treharn. Debbie purchased the hand-crocheted canopy years ago from a woman in Connecticut.*

Debbie added another early mantel in the master bedroom to give warmth to the room which is painted with Old Village 'Rittenhouse Ivory'. The slim feather tree in the corner is simply decorated with reindeer, Santas and cotton batting icicles.

A large make-do chair in the corner holds another Santa's sleigh and reindeer.

Debbie casually draped a vintage woman's dress and shoes on the ladderback chair in the opposite corner.

Debbie liked the look of the rope bed when she and Harry found it in its original dry red paint, but after seeing a similar bed in black, Debbie painted and distressed it to blend with the other pieces in the guestroom.

A large wallpaper box found at Brimfield rests on the middle shelf of the corner cupboard while the Empire period chest of drawers with original hardware displays some of Debbie's coverlets.

The coverlet on the guestroom bed is an early piece dating to the late 19thC. Each holiday season Debbie adds the red long johns for color to her collection of vintage clothing on the peg rack.

Four years ago, Harry's sudden illness served as a wake-up call to each of them. The time off to recover and a new job meant a loss of available free time and vacation days to enjoy their antique hunts. They are careful with their limited free time and rather than buy whatever seems to be popular or 'in', they are more selective and would rather wait for those special opportunities to add to their collections rather than build them in a day. Debbie feels the best part of being an antique collector is the thrill of the hunt!

Chapter 6

Forest and Kathy Oberschlake

If Colonial Williamsburg furnished permanent accommodations on site or offered to whirl a 21stC woman back to the colonial period, Kathy Oberschlake would be the first to volunteer. Since the first visit she and her husband, Forest, made to Williamsburg, Virginia in 2008, Kathy was smitten. Kathy would love to live life as a gentile lady when, as she puts it, "Ladies were ladies", dressed in elegant silk gowns. Kathy has settled for the next best thing – creating a Colonial Williamsburg decorated style home and employing a dressmaker to create a gown so that Kathy can dress in period style during their annual visit to Williamsburg. Even though Forest might wear a polo shirt when visiting Williamsburg, he supports Kathy's interest 100% and contributes by building furniture for their home.

One might think that their 9000+ square foot house on five acres, complete with a large pond, three family horses, and full-time jobs wouldn't allow much spare time for anything else; not the case. Forest is employed as a government contractor with the US Air Force and often travels overseas while Kathy is employed by Chick-fil-A. In addition, for the past 20 years Kathy has participated in 12 horse shows a year riding seven-year-old 'Pretty Persuasion', her American Saddle Bred. Oh . . . did I neglect to mention that Forest and Kathy put up 43 holiday trees each year – many with a theme?

Forest and Kathy built their home in 2001 – the first time! In 2014, during a severe storm with three grandchildren getting ready to shower upstairs, there was a tremendous boom as lightning struck the house blowing out plumbing, the roof, a fireplace, and the upstairs bathroom where one of their grandchildren was waiting. Miraculously, no one was hurt but the house required over $100,000 in repairs.

The door is painted with Colonial Williamsburg 'St. George Red'.

Kathy recalls reading in a magazine that a good decorator chooses one neutral color and enhances it with no more than three complementary colors. Kathy elected an off-white as her base and chose as one of the three 'Tucker Gray' that she used in the entranceway, upstairs halls, and kitchen, which opens to the 'widow's walk' on the second floor.

Kathy first noticed a set of framed prints during a visit to the St. George Tucker home in Williamsburg and mentioned to Forest that she would love to have a set. Forest went on the hunt and located a framed collection of prints depicting the 'Twelve Floral Months of the Year' by Robert Furber, an English nurseryman. Their display on the stairwell makes them visible from either the first or second floor.

The Windsor chair is from The Seraph in Delaware, Ohio. The tree is decorated with fruits and pine cones in the Williamsburg style. An early goat cart beneath carries an Arnett's Santa.

The hanging cupboard on the opposite wall holds a collection of 1768 pewter purchased at The Seraph. Forest designed and built the table beneath that holds a set of pewter chocolate sauce pots.

Kathy chose 'Salmon' from The Seraph *for the living room. The floor cloth was created by Michele Hollick of New Hampshire and purchased for the color of pomegranates in the border that blends beautifully with the walls. Kathy mixed pomegranates, pears, and apples with rusty Angel ornaments with bells on the tree in the living room corner.*

The painting over the mantel is a reproduction oil of a Thomas Gainsborough 1764 painting titled 'Mary Countess Howe'. The mantel is adorned with artificial pineapples, cloved oranges, lemons, holly, and boxwood reminiscent of Williamsburg.

The corner cupboard holds a collection of Queen's pattern pottery purchased at Williamsburg. The pattern is named 'Pot Pourri' after Queen Charlotte.

Forest made the high-backed dry sink of cherry before their first trip to Williamsburg. When he and Kathy moved into the house and embraced the Williamsburg style, Kathy asked Forest to paint the piece to blend with the décor. The doll in the armchair was made by a friend during the 80s when Kathy was enamored with Laura Ashley. The samplers above were rendered by Kathy over the past 20 years and depict different homes in Williamsburg.

Forest made the desk after Kathy noticed a very high-priced piece in a country magazine. They adapted the pattern to add 20 drawers beneath the slant top. Forest painted the surface with a Seraph flat black. A set of three silhouettes hangs on the wall to the left.

For years, Kathy stored a set of Pheasant Company Felicity collector dolls in boxes until she asked Forest to build a dollhouse to showcase her collection. The collection consists of not only Felicity and her furniture but her friend Elizabeth and all Elizabeth's furniture. Forest and Kathy built the 7' high and 6' wide dollhouse with the intention to place it in Kathy's sitting room upstairs; however, the size of the house made that location impossible. The house is a replica of the Colonial Williamsburg President's house and features hardwood floors and nine over six grid windows with glass panes.

The tree in the dining room is decorated with papier-mache ornaments, many purchased at *The Old Farmstead* shop in Beaver Creek, Ohio. Forest purchased the table and chairs prior to his marriage to Kathy.

The paint in the dining room is historic Williamsburg 'Tavern Gold'.

A small settle bench holds some of Kathy's Noah's Ark collection. Numerous other Arks are displayed in the glass front cabinet.

Forest and Kathy's son and his wife planned to discard the large glass front cupboard pictured left when Forest and Kathy offered to take it off their hands! Once Forest added molding and hardware and painted the cupboard using a Seraph dark blue, their son greatly regretted giving the piece up!

Kathy found many of the pewter pieces on the hanging whale tail shelf at The Seraph.

On the small table beneath the spoon rack with drawers, Kathy arranged three Santa figures created by folk artist Pipka Ulviden of Wisconsin.

The kitchen with its 9' ceilings is open and airy with the widow's walk in the second floor hallway.

The cabinets are custom-built cherry in the Shaker style; the countertops are Formica.

The wooden tree beside the island is decorated with miniature stars and gingerbread boys.

Kathy used a pie-drying rack idea she had seen in Williamsburg and instead of pies uses the rack to display a variety of fruit on pewter plates.

The tree beside the built-in desk is filled with snowflakes, candy canes, Santa boots, and gingerbread boy ornaments.

The open shelf holds a chocolate sauce set used in the 18thC to melt blocks of chocolate to make sauce.

A Ragon House Belsnickel in gray cape nestles in the corner on the counter.

Kathy used a vintage hanging scale to create a small holiday vignette.

The kitchen cabinetry was designed to allow Kathy space for decorating on top. Each space is filled with greenery, small trees, Santa figures, and numerous Longaberger baskets.

The Santa pictured above left is another created by folk artist Pipka Ulviden.

A small back hallway provides the ideal spot for a bucket bench and tavern sign.

Above a library table in the back hallway a French map depicts the five rivers in Colonial Williamsburg. The Christmas tree is filled with miniature Colonial Williamsburg figure ornaments.

The mantel in the family room is decorated with greenery, lights, and three Ragon House Belsnickels. The paintings above are reproductions and titled 'Mr. Minor and Son' and 'Mrs. Minor and Daughter'.

Kathy loves to collect early editions of Christmas books or miniatures of children's holiday stories which she adds as accents around the house.

Every window in the house is decorated with a Williamsburg cluster of greens, fruit, and artificial magnolia leaves.

The tree in the corner is surrounded by Kathy's polar bear collection that began as she shopped in Waynesville, Ohio and found a mother and cub in the window. The shop owner refused to dicker on the price or separate the pieces, so Kathy walked away. On a later trip she was devastated when she passed the shop window and the bears were gone. As it turned out, Forest and their granddaughter had purchased the pair as a holiday gift for Kathy. That was all it took to begin a collection which now numbers over thirty.

Forest made the desk and the hanging wall shelf in the corner.

Above the desk hangs a print of The Bodleian Plate – a copper plate dating to the mid-18thC that shows what Williamsburg looked like.

The sleigh and Santa is an Arnett's creation.

Forest built the cantback cupboard which Kathy fills with Pipka Santas.

Forest and Kathy purchased the four poster bed unfinished over 25 years ago. The crocheted canopy was ordered from a magazine. The coverlet in sage green was recently traded out from a dark blue to give the room a softer look. The walls are painted with the same 'Salmon' as in the living room.

The small table at the foot of the bed is the base of a low boy. Kathy was able to purchase it at a greatly reduced price because a back leg was broken; she knew that Forest could remedy the break. Kathy draped Santa's pajamas, socks, and night cap over the reproduction Windsor chair alongside.

Forest and Kathy purchased the highboy at The Seraph; Forest refinished the piece adding period hardware. The three-drawer chest on top was one designed and built by Forest.

The oil painting above the faux fireplace was found at The Seraph. The tree is decorated with primitive joint Santa figures and rusty hearts.

Ebenezer Scrooge is Forest's favorite Christmas story, so it is only fitting that the tree in his study is filled with Charles Dicken's ornaments. Each year Kathy finds a different ornament to add to his collection. The figures beneath the tree are Byers' Christmas carolers.

The game room houses three more trees, each with a theme. The tree shown right is the Ohio State tree, their son's alma mater.

The tree in the dormer window is their granddaughter's tree filled with horse ornaments, while in the foreground their toddler grandson's tree is filled with Mickey Mouse and little animal ornaments; his favorite is the squirrel.

Kathy's love of horses and competition in horse shows make the decorations on the tree in her Sitting Room a perfect opportunity each year for gift giving by family and friends.

The patriotic decorated tree in the landing upstairs is a throwback to Kathy's earlier pre-Colonial Williamsburg days, but she didn't have the heart to change it. The drop leaf table is early and constructed with square nails. Kathy arranged the vignette around the table as a 'tavern' area using pewter tankards, a clay pipe, a tavern sign, and gameboards.

Across the hallway is another tree filled with snowmen figures.

I asked Kathy about her future plans, and the very first thing she answered was a 44th tree for 2017! She is also finishing a series of Williamsburg samplers that she has worked on since 2011. Since the lightning strike, Kathy finished repainting the house entirely and looks forward to the warmer months when she can work in her perennial gardens.

When I asked if she was done, she said that's what Forest wonders. He just says, "Honey, tell me when you're done!"

Chapter 7

Vincent and Lisa DiLeo

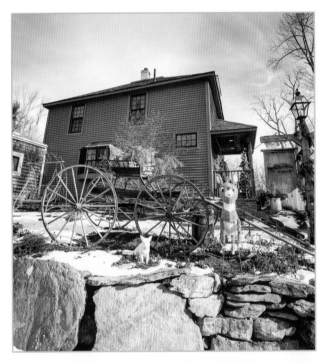

After sixteen years of remodeling their mid-1800s farmhouse in Leicester, Massachusetts, Vincent and Lisa DiLeo are ready to move on to what Lisa refers to as her 'dream house' – a saltbox colonial like the one her cousin Mary Riani owns. (Mary's home was featured in an earlier book, *When Autumn Leaves Start to Fall*).

Vinnie is a contractor and electrician by trade, the perfect combination to take on the extensive work they've tackled on their farmhouse over the years. They have upgraded electrical and plumbing/heating systems, not to mention two additions. How they can think of leaving their Great Room shown at the end of their chapter is beyond my understanding!

Lisa is a homemaker in every sense of the word; after the importance of family, she will tell you that more than anything she loves to enjoy her home as a stay-at-home mom to the last of their three children.

Artist Susan Dwyer painted the mural in the front entrance which complements the trim paint from Benjamin Moore, 'Winter Meadow'.

Vinnie added wide pine flooring throughout the house from Carlisle Flooring in New Hampshire.

Vinnie added the beams to the living room using wood from an old mill in nearby Hopedale, Massachusetts. Lisa says they barely ever use the room but she never tires of sitting and gazing at everything in it.

I have yet to encounter anyone who has experienced Lisa's success with Craig's List. The high back fireside chairs are a Craig's List find, originally made by Angel House in Brookfield, Massachusetts. This chapter

will probably sound like an advertisement for Craig's List as Lisa has had extraordinary success, despite the occasional long trip to pick up a treasure.

Lisa purchased the large 19thC red settle at the Sturbridge Antique Center. A hanging lantern and small folk art Santa figure curls up in one corner.

The writing desk chair with comb back was another Craig's List find. The window treatments were purchased at Jackie's Primitives.

Lisa loves horses and displays a number of children's riding and platform horse pull toys.

Lisa found the instructions for building a faux mantel in my earlier book, A Simpler Time. She painted the mantel 'Pumpkin' from The Seraph to contrast with the Benjamin Moore 'Sage Green' on the trim.

Lisa found the robin's egg blue schoolmaster's desk and spinning wheel at a local antique shop.

The gas stove was used to supplement the heating system prior to the addition of the Great Room where most of their time is spent. The upholstered chair is from Angel House.

Lisa uses one side of the chimney as a rack to display her bonnets, an early lantern, skates, and Sweet Annie. The sign above – 'Winter Time Traditions – Family' speaks to her heart.

Susan Dwyer painted the large mural on the fireplace wall in the dining room. I could look at this wall for hours.

Lisa loves the look of Colonial Williamsburg and uses artificial fruit and greenery to create a mantel indicative of the style. The use of artificial pieces allows Lisa to enjoy the decorations long after the holiday season ends.

Lisa chose a Seraph paint 'Pumpkin' for the trim in the room and loves how the reproduction blue/gray dry sink almost 'shimmers' against the wall. While Lisa likes early bowls with dry paint, she never walks away from a dough bowl with attic surface when the price is right.

The kitchen cabinetry is painted with Benjamin Moore 'Sage Green' and accented with homespun red-checked curtains.

Lisa cooks daily on the Elmira cast iron stove nestled in the brick alcove.

Lisa purchased the farm table at Ye Country Mercantile in Sturbridge; it is a crafted piece by Jeff Dana, who exhibits kitchen design at the Mercantile.

The 19thC jelly cupboard was found at the Sturbridge Antique Center and affords shelf space for Lisa's collection of mortars and pestles, pantry boxes, and a wonderful spice box pictured on the bottom shelf, shown left.

The addition off the dining room began as a sunroom, but soon became a four-season Great Room roomy enough to accommodate their combined large family.

Vinnie planed and sanded boards from the old mill in Hopedale for the beams and ceiling. He used half bricks for the flooring.

The Santa on the mantel is from Arnett's. The picture of a horse drawn sleigh was a gift to Lisa from Vinnie one Christmas.

The cupboards and racks are filled with redware, treen, sifters, measures, and firkins.

The child's sled on the chest dates to the 19thC.

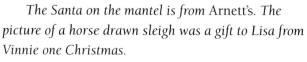

Lisa has placed the vintage child's rocking horse on a 19thC grain bin that she purchased at the Sturbridge Antique Center.

The large Santa in front of the red make-do chair is another Arnett's creation. The large table is known as a settle table where the family gathers during every holiday.

Lisa painted the trim in Vinnie's den with 'New England Red' from Olde Century.

The pie safe in the corner was yet another Craig's List find, but this one almost put Vinnie over the edge. After a long drive, they found the elderly gentleman selling the piece so lonely that he wanted Lisa and Vinnie to drive him around so he could show them his town. Lisa felt compassion for the man and agreed, much to Vinnie's dismay!

The horse pictured beside the tree comes with another soft-hearted Lisa story. After finding the horse on Craig's List, Lisa visited the seller, whose home was not only lovely but filled with exquisite early antiques. The woman was downsizing to a condominium, a move that Lisa thought she might regret since she would be forced to sell all her treasures. Lisa did her best to talk the nice woman out of selling everything and to this day wonders where she is and hopes things worked out well.

Lisa purchased the master bedroom bed from The Seraph; *the quilt was purchased from a retail store and chosen because of its vibrant colors.*

The quilt and coverlet on the guestroom bed are newer pieces and were also chosen for their vibrant colors.

Lisa admits she is more content with her home. If she feels like a change, she switches rugs which gives a room a new look with minimal effort.

I appreciate that Lisa is ready for a change after 16 years but . . . if THIS gorgeous country farmhouse is their practice run, WHAT will the next house look like!? I guess we'll have to wait and see!

Chapter 8

❧ ✿ ❧

Jack and Betsy Merklein

Everyone loves a success story and I've just heard another from one of our kindred spirits! After speaking with Betsy Merklein of Manassas, Virginia, and listening to her creative path from macaroni and cutting boards to owner of a successful country shop for 31 years, it occurred to me that we country decorators may each possess a creative gene and that gene may be what binds us together. We each have a knack for creativity and sometimes channel it in different directions, oftentimes along a journey that takes us far from where the path began. Not only is Betsy's career path an interesting story, the account of how she and her husband Jack ended up married for 40 years is like something out of a novel.

Betsy grew up in Crisfield, Maryland along the Chesapeake Bay. Jack, though born in Crisfield, moved with his military family and returned to Crisfield as a teenager. Jack and Betsy became friends in middle school, and although they never dated in school, they remained close friends during Jack's years at West Point and Betsy's years at Penn State. Jack was about to graduate from The U. S. Military Academy when he parted ways with his girlfriend. As he did not want to miss the social events associated with his graduation, Jack contacted Betsy to see if she would accompany him. Six months later they were engaged and six months after that they married.

Jack is Director of Knowledge Management at an international non-profit. When not traveling or at his

desk, he can be found in Betsy's shop, *Personally Yours*, in Occoquan, Virginia, selling everything from dip mixes to hand lotions. He is also Betsy's right-hand man at shows, settling payments and gathering receipts for Betsy's purchases long after Betsy has moved on to the next booth. Like the sign in shops that reads, "Your husband called and said you can buy whatever you want", Betsy admits that Jack will say, "Why buy one when 10 is better!"

A large Arnett's Santa sits comfortably in an early dump cart on the front steps. Betsy placed a tall artificial feather tree for him to lean against.

Betsy enjoys the advantage of being a shop owner and having access to items she might also choose to use in her home. The wreath is from Sullivan's Florals, to which Betsy added a crafted reindeer by Olde Time Santas.

The front entrance opens to an area large enough to accommodate their 8' artificial tree.

Betsy has discovered ways to alter the large open floor plan of their 20-year-old home to give each space a homey country feel. Walking straight ahead once inside the front door, a visitor enters the kitchen with a large family room attached, where Jack and Betsy spend most of their time.

The mantel is filled with carved Santa figures by Joy Hall. Betsy's shop is the only one that markets her carvings.

During the early years of their marriage Betsy began her career by handcrafting items she sold to military wives. Betsy grew up with a dad whose hobby was woodworking, and Betsy spent hours in the garage with him developing an obsession for wood. Although she graduated from college with a culinary degree with the intent of becoming a chef, Betsy redirected her creative genes from food to wood and began to make crafts to sell, some of which she cringes at the thought of today – for example, noodle decoupage on old cutting boards! They were an instant hit with the military wives and despite the fact she had never picked up a paint brush, Betsy moved on to painting tavern signs. Another instant hit!

By the time Betsy and Jack reached Virginia 31 years ago, Betsy wielded a band saw and rented space in a craft shop in Occoquan where she met another crafter, Ann Sweeny, an artist who later joined her at *Personally Yours*. Following a few years on the craft show circuit, they opened their first store in Occoquan where they remained business partners until 2014 when Ann retired and Betsy moved *Personally Yours* to its present location.

The mural of the Potomac River was painted by Ann Sweeny.

The mustard and blue cupboard repurposed from old wood was found in Pennsylvania. A half drop leaf table with a 22" single board drop holds a large collection of graduated stoneware crocks.

The walls of the sunroom, often used as a dining area, are painted with Sherwin-Williams 'Cardboard'. The tablecloth is a king-size bed coverlet from Family Heirloom Weavers. The Christmas place settings hold special meaning to Betsy as they were a gift from her dad shortly before he passed away 15 years ago. The 19thC pine jelly cupboard, a Delaware piece, is constructed with 1" thick boards. On top are displayed old crocks, Joy Hall carved snowmen, and stairway spindles which serve as the base for small feather trees.

Betsy found the small blue/green cupboard in a shop in Lititz, Pennsylvania. The bowls are from Colonial Woodworks in Frederick, Maryland and hold Betsy's collection of butter paddles.

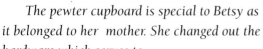

The pewter cupboard is special to Betsy as it belonged to her mother. She changed out the hardware which serves to match the piece with the rest of the room's décor.

In the sitting area of the sunroom, David T. Smith redware mingles with Santas made by Debbee Thibault.

The kitchen counters are Corian which Betsy hopes to update when time permits. Above the cupboards, Betsy has arranged Arnett's Santas, a large early trencher, and small feather trees sitting in early crocks.

Betsy's island is actually the stove which she hopes to move someday. While the removable Corian top offers a great amount of work and display space, it makes preparing meals almost impossible — not that Betsy is complaining!

In the corner of the counter, the three early cutting boards were painted with Santa figures by Ann Sweeny.

The windowsill above the sink holds three Joy Hall Santas and a small brush tree that Betsy has placed in early bobbins for a base.

Betsy uses an old sugar mold as a base for small votive candles.

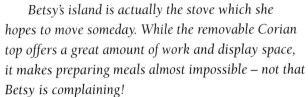

A feather tree stands on a stack of small cutting boards at one end of the island.

The counter at one end of the kitchen looks into the sunroom area. A vintage cutting board holds a pair of fabric reindeer by Barbara Stein; they stand behind a Santa carved by folk artist Bobby Hoffman of Missouri. The small skater's lantern is an early piece which Betsy illuminates with a flameless votive candle by Marsh Homestead.

The painted peel is another piece created by Ann Sweeny; it leans against an early grain bin found in Lancaster, Pennsylvania.

Betsy enjoys the good fortune to be able to collect Joy Hall's carvings and has been doing so for almost 20 years. By adding two or three a year, she has accumulated an impressive collection. The large pewter cupboard affords her the space to make an immediate statement as a visitor enters the front door.

What an inspiring success story! Betsy has traveled from noodle boards to owner of a business, Personally Yours, for the past 31 years, now in its third and largest location in Occoquan, Virginia.

Betsy shared that if her mother had known that she and Jack would marry within a year after giving Betsy permission to attend events at West Point, she might have thought twice. Who would have guessed! But then who would have guessed that a successful business could begin with macaroni!

Personally Yours is located at 402 Mill Street in historic Occoquan, Virginia. The new location occupies two floors with eight rooms offering an extensive line of home accessories and seasonal gifts including reproduction furniture and country accessories.

The shop is open 7 days a week and offers a number of special events each year, including Spring Fling, an annual anniversary sale and a holiday open house.

Betsy maintains a website www.pyinc.biz.

Her telephone number is 703-494-8683.

Chapter 9

❧ ❀ ❧

Jim and Kathy Gilliland

Kathy and Jim Gilliland of Ogden, Illinois were first introduced to 'country' by some friends who made items which they would sell out of their home. At the time, Kathy was a registered nurse and Jim was employed by the local utility company. As soon as they saw the country pieces, Kathy fell in love with the look and shortly after was riding her bike past an older house in the process of being remodeled. It was primitive and the look touched Kathy so that she walked up to the owner and said, "Hi. I'm Kathy Gilliland and I need to know you." The owners were very gracious people who took Kathy under their wing and introduced her to their circle of primitive friends.

Kathy admits that she and Jim are relatively late bloomers, but they jumped right in and began making country pieces and remodeling their home. Kathy has since opened a shop, *The Country Lamb*, which is showcased at the end of the chapter.

Their front porch is filled with primitive finds, from a goat cart to a 'winter wagon' that Kathy saves just for the holiday season to preserve it. She enjoys complementing primitives with gourds and of course plenty of greenery during the holidays.

The walls in the living room are painted with Sherwin-Williams 'Camelback' and trimmed with Shaker Village called 'Trusty Brown'.

Jim and Kathy found an old pumpkin painted fireplace front in Indiana and adapted it to their living room. Jim extended the mantel and sides then bricked the hearth and opening. Kathy dry brushed the surface with black paint to age it and added a crane and old kettle for effect. The child's chair was purchased from Linda Miller of Miller Antiques in Carroll, Ohio.

Jim and Kathy's friends, JJ and Jody Coffin, whose home was featured in Simply Country Gardens and It's the Most Wonderful Time of the Year, taught them how to lay wide pine plank flooring and have been instrumental in guiding Jim and Kathy on their remodeling path. Kathy readily admits to her perfectionist nature and confesses her frustration when installing wide pine plank flooring. She finally accepted the fact that country décor isn't always perfect.

The couch was from Johnston-Benchworks and is reupholstered in a historic flame pattern fabric from The Seraph. The shelf above holds two early straw-stuffed bears – one of Kathy's favorite collections.

In nearby Bloomington, the third Sunday of each month features a large flea market where Jim and Kathy purchased the early bench in blue that they use as a coffee table.

The large two-door 19thC cupboard with red paint was found at a shop in Champlain. Seated in the blue checked wingback chair is another early bear, while a straw-filled doll purchased from Linda Miller hangs on the door front. The lamp on the side table is from Katie's Lighthouse. Jim and Kathy discovered that changing all the lighting in the house as a first step in remodeling offered an instant country improvement to the overall feel of each room.

Jim and Kathy found the dry sink in front of the window at Sweet Annie Primitives, a wonderful shop in Bishop Hill, Illinois. A pair of Santa figures from Ragon House silhouettes against the window; the early treen bowl is filled with blackened beeswax Santas. Tucked in the corner, an early ladder holds vintage linens, one of Jim and Kathy's first finds raising a number of questions from their children who weren't quite sure where all of this decorating was headed.

Jim and Kathy found the farm table and chairs at a shop in Tuscola, Illinois. When these photographs were taken, Kathy was about to paint the base black to match the chairs while Jim planned to sand and refinish the top.

Kathy arranges a grouping in the center of the table of beeswax flameless taper candles from Marsh Homestead Antiques.

Jim and Kathy bought the corner cupboard unfinished and Kathy painted it a deep red to give it a country look. She uses a dark stain and then a dry black paint to darken it.

Kathy didn't care for the color of the tall chimney cupboard but liked the style. She distressed the piece and darkened it with dark stain to give it a 'dirtier' appearance.

The iron candlestick on top of the bowl rack was made by blacksmith Kathy Nugent of Kansas.

Jim and Kathy purchased the two-piece cupboard at the Homesteaders on the Prairie Show *from antique dealer Linda Miller. It is an east coast piece which had been painted by Sally Whims and Kathy couldn't believe their good fortune that it was still available at the end of the show. Although Jim was happy to drive the hour long trip home and return with their truck, friends came to the rescue and helped Jim and Kathy get it home.*

A small alcove off the dining room once joined the house and Kathy's shop prior to Kathy moving her shop to a small building in the backyard. Their son suggested she remodel the space and create a buttery; it is now one of Kathy's favorite spots in the house!

Jim and Kathy purchased the dry sink from Jimmy Rochelle in Tennessee. Kathy liked the style but not the surface, so with the help of Linda Miller, they once again hired Sally Whims to paint it. Sally mentioned that she received many offers for the piece.

Jim affixed horizontal boards to the walls and Kathy selected Olde Century 'Old Ivory' paint and 'Linen White' for the ceiling and trim.

One step down from the kitchen, the family room was once the garage and now is the room where everyone gathers.

The bench in front of the couch features a single-board top and was found in Ohio. The log cabin is from Sweet Annie Primitives. The treen bowl holds a flameless hand-poured pillar candle from Marsh Homestead Antiques.

Standing on the top of the early one drawer work table at the end of the couch is a primitive chicken feeder which Kathy has filled with gourds.

The walls are painted with Sherwin-Williams 'Camelback'. The trim is 'Trusty Brown'.

The small cupboard in the corner holds an iron candleholder and charger made by Kathy Nugent.

Kathy leaned a weathered barn door as a backdrop behind the early farm worktable. The red chest beneath the table was Jim's grandfather's old tool chest.

Her large collection of early German and newer sheep gaze from a small wall cupboard.

Kathy loves Civil War history and purchased the period musket over the fireplace.

Kathy found the early lidded doughbox in dry red paint at The Seville Antique Center in Ohio.

Kathy's countertops are wood and contrast with the wooden backsplash painted with 'Old Ivory'.

The small shelf and drawer seen bottom left is new, however the tin-lidded jars and apothecary are old.

The guestroom remains the only room that Jim has not replaced carpeting with pine flooring. The bed is covered with a Family Heirloom Weavers coverlet; Kathy painted the bed black for an older look. The walls are painted with Olde Century 'Linen White'.

A rocking chair holds a pair of very early quilts which Kathy displays only during the holidays. A treasured early baby quilt dating to the Civil War is displayed in the box on the chest.

In a second guestroom, an early wagon with original red paint and metal wheels holds four vintage bears and an early doll with a bonnet.

The desk at the foot of the bed is a sawbuck table found in Indiana. Kathy placed an early child's reading book, candlestick, and lantern on top. The chair holds a large early flag.

The table lights on the large desk in the corner are from Carriage House Lighting in Ohio. Old bonnets and a purse handcrafted in Kentucky are displayed on the rack above an early chest. The tool box holds a horse from Arnett's.

Jim and Kathy thought their original master bedroom was too small so they added a new bedroom on the back of the house and converted the old one into a sitting room suite!

The walls are painted with 'Olde Ivory' but interestingly take on different colors in each room depending upon the light.

Jim and Kathy found the desk at a show in Arthur, Illinois.

The large armoire below is used to hold clothing. Kathy used a discarded old drawer to create a small display for miniature brush trees and Santa figures from Ragon House.

Folk artist Angela Hillstrom of Cloth and Hand in Tennessee made the Civil War figures that Kathy purchased at The Appalachian Museum Show in Tennessee.

The small cupboard above the ladderback chair was the first antique Kathy purchased.

The chest at the foot of the bed is from The Seraph.

Kathy found the cradle at a shop in Missouri and uses it to showcase early dolls: a broom doll and a straw-filled doll.

Angela Hillstrom made the folk art ornaments on the feather tree displayed in a small wooden stand with fence that Kathy found in Tennessee.

The bed cover is accented with a Family Heirloom Weavers throw. The lighting is from Carriage House and the Santa from Ragon House.

A dry sink repurposed to a vanity carries the country theme into the master bath.

Considering Kathy's passion for Civil War history, the log cabin that purportedly originated from General Sheridan's hometown in Ohio was a must-have. Jim and Kathy purchased the logs from Curry's Antiques in Lancaster, Ohio, and Jim and their son, Tony, assembled the logs, added the roof and built the porch. Jody Coffin, having chinked three cabins of her own, taught Kathy the chinking process. An old barn door was added adorned with a simple bough of greenery and small gourds. It's not surprising that the cabin is called 'The General' in honor of General Sheridan.

A section of tobacco fence rests on a weathered bench and holds greens alongside two early grinding wheels.

Kathy uses the cabin to decorate and opens it to customers during special events for her shop.

Kathy's shop, The Country Lamb, is located in the building adjoining the cabin.

The Country Lamb is open by chance or appointment and Kathy suggests a call ahead to be sure. Kathy may be reached via email at Jimkathygilliland@gmail.com or by phone 217-582-2575.

Kathy and Jim might have gotten a late start and admit, "You can't just snap your fingers and have instant country", but from what I can see they've earned an A+ at catching up!

Chapter 10

❧ ◆ ❧

John and Rebecca Dickenscheidt

In 1998, when John and Rebecca Dickenscheidt built their home in Tinley Park, Illinois, Rebecca admits they didn't have any specific style in mind. She looks back now and realizes perhaps she is a "little late to the game" of antiques and collecting but would like to learn more about identifying authentic pieces. To achieve the country look, Rebecca selects the finest-quality artisan-made reproduction pieces as a backdrop for an incredible collection of folk art. Their home is like touring a folk art museum, and Rebecca's collection is so extensive that I have included artist's websites as references at the end of her chapter. If you enjoy folk art, you'll love this tour.

John and Rebecca are both from the Chicago area and both work in finance: John is with CommScope and Rebecca works in investment banking research. Their time and 'hobby' at this point revolve around their three children who are active participants in band and various sports.

The dry sink inside the front door was built by David T. Smith. On top is a tree decorated with tiny painted signs by Wendy Stys-Van Eimeren and gingerbread boys by folk artist Angela Hillstrom of Tennessee.

Their house features an open floor plan which Rebecca finds difficult to work with, but she enjoys the openness the vaulted ceilings afford.

The wing-back chair in the living room is from The Seraph. The Santa holding a crow on the windowsill was crafted by Paulette Andrews.

The white cupboard from California is made with old wood.

The house on top was made by folk artist Harold Turpin. The hanging basket made by Linda Searcy is decorated with an angel crafted by Angela Hillstrom. A snowman from Arnett's Country Store stands on the coffee table.

Displayed over the comb back Windsor chair crafted by Bill Wallick is a set of silhouettes of John and Rebecca's three children made by Kolene Spicher.

Rebecca was drawn to the painted angels by Kathy Graybill on the doors of the vintage blue cupboard. Standing on top is a Santa from Arnett's . The lamp is from The Tin Peddler while the shelf above is from Primitiques in Pennsylvania.

The gameboards on the stairway wall are all new pieces hand-painted by different folk artists. The large blue painted board is by Primitiques.

Rebecca used crocheted garlands of red wool to decorate the large tree at the foot of the stairs. The tree is filled with small ornaments crafted by Angela Hillstrom and Kay Cloud.

Angela made the Santa and elf pictured above.

Kay Cloud made the angel and the bear pictured below left.

A narrow wall between the living and dining rooms allows just the right amount of space for a huntboard in black over red. Kathy Graybill painted the Chadwick Inn tavern sign; the lamp is a Lt. Moses Willard; the Santa from Tom Panetta who hand sculpts seasonal creations under the name Krisnick. A basket filled with black dolls by Kay Cloud sits beneath the table.

The cherry table in the dining room was built by Amish craftsmen. The table linen is from Family Heirloom Weavers. The large trencher is an early piece.

The large pine pie safe holds an early doughbox with dry red original wash where Rebecca displays another Arnett's Santa.

The late Arthur Glazier painted the wonderful farmer and his wife on the bottom of drawers believed to have been taken from an old general store counter.

The snowman pictured below right was made by Becky Carney. The brown twig tree is filled with an assortment of country ornaments.

The craftsman who made the apple green corner cupboard used old wood and then applied early wallpaper to the back to further age the piece.

Linda Searcy made the basket on top; Tom Panetta sculpted the Santas and reindeer.

Rebecca purchased the stocking made from an early coverlet from Linda Heard, owner of Lindowens, a shop in New York. The white stocking is from Arnett's; the red from Kay Cloud. The rye basket is an antique.

David T. Smith designed and built the kitchen. After an initial house call to measure and fact find, John and Rebecca visited Smith's workshop to select colors. John and Rebecca then had a contractor remove the original cabinetry and provide Smith with a blank palette. The end result is a 'Collected Kitchen' with several free-standing cupboards should John and Rebecca decide to move. The cupboard shown right is grain- painted. The plates on the lighted narrow shelf are from David T. Smith. The snowman is by Tom Panetta.

The kitchen's design is intended to optimize storage and conceal appliances. The mustard cupboard left is called an appliance cupboard as it houses the microwave, blender, toaster, and other small appliances. The cherry cupboard conceals the double oven while the slate blue piece hides the refrigerator.

Folk artist Tammy Jias made the gingerbread boys hanging on checked fabric over the kitchen sink. The small feather tree on the counter is decorated with miniature stockings.

The small feather tree on the counter stands in an early firkin and is decorated with little candy canes.

David and Lana Testa of Winterberry Primitives made the noodle board and treen plates that cover the stovetop. The grain scoop is early.

The wood carved Belsnickel was made by Marlene Dusbiber, a Michigan artist. John and Cathy Schneeman painted the storage glass jars.

Rebecca placed a hand-painted sign by Heidi Howard over the vaulted beam in the kitchen. The animals were made by Angela Hillstrom, the Santa figure by Jane Wallace.

Kathy Graybill painted the fireboard that depicts a country house.

Kay Cloud made all the trees displayed on the mantel. She attached bay leaves to some giving the display a homey aroma. The 'Merry Christmas' sign was painted by Tammy Belliveau of Mill River Primitives.

The hanging cupboard and chair are by Primitiques. The snowman on the chair was crafted by Marlene Robertson of Village Primitives; the stocking was made by Kay Cloud.

The holiday framed theorem was painted by Carole Behrer. Lana Testa made the snowmen alongside.

On top of the small cupboard stands a Santa crafted by Becky Carney.

Tucked in the corner to the left of the fireplace, a red cupboard crafted by Good Intent Farm holds a small document box made by Ohio folk artist Kenneth James. Above it, the stockings are by Arnett's, the basket by Linda Searcy, the Santa figure by Dru Ann Jeffries, and the lamp by Carriage House Lighting.

David T. Smith made the collector's cupboard that is ideal for displaying Rebecca's collection of pin keeps, many of which were made by Kay Cloud, Norma Schneeman, and Barbara Young. Kolene Spicher painted John and Rebecca's three children in a 19thC primitive style.

David T. Smith made the large black/green pewter cupboard displayed on the opposite side of the room. Some of his redware plates are seen in the glass front top; a snowman by Kimberly Bouffard sits on the shelf below.

The sign above the sleigh bed in the master bedroom is another Kathy Graybill creation. The Windsor settle at the foot of the bed holds a Santa crafted by Mandy Fischer of Bittersweet Folk Art.

Heidi Howard painted the 'Hats Made to Order' sign on old wood. It hangs above a jelly cupboard made by Benner's Woodworking. The tree standing in front is filled with miniature hat boxes by Angela Hillstrom. She added a small bell on the bottom of each tiny hat box. John and Cathy Schneeman designed the mustard painted lamp.

Another Kathy Graybill sign hangs on the wall beneath a Linda Searcy basket and Arnett's snowman.

Rebecca feels as though a whole new world has opened up to her with Pinterest, Facebook, and selling sites such as Primitive Handmades Mercantile and Early Work Mercantile, to name a few. These sites allow Rebecca access to a wealth of folk artists and enable her to create a home which is truly 'a work of art'.

Chapter 11

⌒ ✦ ⌒

Greg and Patty Kiefer

Greg and Patty Kiefer's life-style and priorities have not changed much since I featured their Massillon, Ohio home in 2009.

Greg and Patty are both retired and still involved in volunteer work with their church and Meals on Wheels. 'Family' is Greg and Patty's number one priority, so in the past few years when Patty's sister became seriously ill, Greg and Patty have assumed responsibility as her primary caregivers.

Their home has changed little since 2009 because 20 years ago when they began collecting antiques and built a house with period features, they purchased high-end antiques from reputable dealers and elected to keep the pieces rather than 'upgrade' or exchange.

The mantel in the living room dates to the early 1800s; it was purchased from the late Nancy Kalin. Patty painted it with Old Heritage 'Linen Cupboard White'. The pewter chargers are early and exhibit a rich, dark patina. The standing tin candleholder was purchased from Marjorie Staufer and is sand-weighted. The ladderback chair is another purchase from Nancy Kalin; it dates to the late 1700s.

The unsigned portrait is from a home in Worcester, Massachusetts and was purchased from Phyllis Yob, a dealer at Seville Antique Mall.

The brick on the hearth was salvaged from an early house in Cleveland and arranged in a pattern recreating a 19thC hearth.

The blue Queen Anne chair belonged to Greg's grandparents which they purchased when they first

emigrated to the United States from Denmark in the late 1800s. When Greg and Patty had it reupholstered, the upholsterer left some of the original horsehair.

Each of the trees reflects a theme. This is the family tree and holds ornaments of significance to Greg and Patty. A family tradition of hanging each baby's first rattle has been carried down; Greg's and their two son's rattles hold a spot of prominence. The gold foil angel tree topper was purchased in the first year of Greg and Patty's marriage 55 years ago.

The pine corner cupboard is 19thC and retains its twelve original panes of glass and pegged shelves. The candlestand was one of the first antiques Greg and Patty purchased. The miniature framed watercolor is unsigned and was purchased from antique dealer Dan Dennis.

The tall clock is signed 'Riley Whiting' from Winchester, Connecticut. It retains its original pewter hands and wooden geared movements. A handwritten note in old brown ink on the back is dated December 1811. It indicates that the clock was purchased from a home in 'Rockland, Maine'. It is a 30 hour clock in original red grain-painted wash.

The desk belonged to Greg's mother and was presented to her from her parents when she graduated from high school.

A vintage Persian wool rug adds color to the corner and complements the tones in the early remnant on the table. The table is a stretcher base New England tavern table dating to the 18thC; the top is pine and the legs are maple. Resting on top is a copy of A Christmas Carol by Charles Dickens dating to 1867.

Purchased from Turnbaugh Antiques at the Seville Antique Mall, the New England swing leg table below the windows features a single-board top measuring 20" wide. It is a Hepplewhite table with tapered legs and original red wash.

The holiday coverlet on the dining area table was purchased at a former country store.

Greg gave the stepback pictured below to Patty as a Christmas gift. Patty uses the open shelves to display numerous early redware and manganese crocks. The Windsor chair is 18thC and was purchased from Marjorie Staufer's home.

A 19thC jelly cupboard with original red wash is one of Patty's favorites; it was purchased from Marjorie Staufer in Medina, Ohio. The sampler above the jelly cupboard is stitched in red and green threads is signed 'Ellen Kimball 11 year ace 1843'.

Patty uses a small alcove between the kitchen and Keeping Room to place a settle purchased from Marie Faren at Seville. Although it is not an early piece, Patty was drawn

to its size and form. The early basket is called a kettle basket and was purchased from Andi Teter at Seville. The vintage quilt is brought out only at holiday season. Patty first noticed the quilt at a show and felt it was too costly. She then attended a second show and noted it again. When she saw it a third time in Seville, she thought she had better not risk waiting any longer! The small dry red painted cupboard was also found at Seville in Matt Ereshman's booth.

The tree in the Keeping Room is the country tree and is decorated with primitive ornaments. The pewter plates are from Marjorie Staufer; the mirrored sconces are new pieces but blend beautifully with the period pieces.

The hand-forged ratchet loom light is from Bobbi Pries. The skillet and the crane are from Marjorie Staufer and date to the 18thC.

I loved the original blue painted candlebox when I first saw it almost 10 years ago and it hasn't lost its appeal as far as I'm concerned!

At the end of the couch in the Keeping Room, a 19thC treen vessel stands on top of a table dating to the 1800s.

Just inside the door, a Shaker table with original pulls and pegs holds an early stoneware jug lamp. The shade is old and made of thick burlap similar to jute. Patty purchased the lamp and shade from Esther Caswell. The provenance on the jug shows it was from Vermont and was used to hold and store syrup.

Patty purchased the small dry red wash hanging cupboard 20 years ago from Esther Caswell and could have sold it over and over since then. The table beneath is a perfect fit for the corner nook leading into the kitchen.

Patty purchased the table from antique dealer Carol Schulman; the Linsey-Woolsey remnant on top is also from Esther Coswell.

One room Greg and Patty did change was a bedroom after finding an old mantel with original white paint at a show in Hudson, Ohio. Greg and Patty purchased it and the fireboard from dealer Mike Kellogg.

Each holiday season Patty adds a bucket of greens to the colorful stool beside the bed. The fabric on the stool is an old coverlet and the colors are ideal for the season.

The coverlet on the bed dates to the 1800s. Two simple stockings are added for a holiday touch.

This holiday tree is decorated with strings of popcorn created by her first grade students when Patty taught elementary school. The cupboard behind was original to the school where Patty taught and holds special memories for Patty. The cupboard was offered to her before the school was razed as the children referred to it as 'Old Mother Hubbard's Cupboard'.

When Greg and Patty's sons were younger, the boys asked if they could use a string of lights which they promptly added to an old wreath and hung over the garage for years. Seemingly at the end of

its days, Patty thought it best to display it on an Adirondack chair and get one more year out of it.

With caregiving, volunteer work, and traveling to see family, Greg and Patty are not out on the antique trail as much as they once were. Patty put it beautifully when she said, "We are still transforming, but more gently."

Chapter 12

Mark Judkins

Mark Judkins of Buxton, Maine has always felt a fondness for antiques, but when he and his former wife became overseers of The Marrett House in Standish, Maine, it clinched the deal. The Marrett House, built in 1789, was owned by the Preservation of Historic New England Antiquities. In 1989 and 1990, Mark and his former wife lived in the ell of the house in exchange for conducting tours and maintaining the well-known perennial gardens.

Two years later, Mark purchased a 1978 reproduction saltbox on a wooded acre. The house was decorated with blue wallpaper and orange shag carpeting throughout; almost immediately Mark began to create a country style apropos for a saltbox.

Mark comes from a long line of teachers; his grandmother taught in a one-room schoolhouse. Mark has been a teacher for 32 years and currently teaches third grade in South Portland, the second largest city in Maine. Mark has little 'down' time which is how he likes it! On weekends he works at Guy and Debbie Paulin's shop, *Country Collectibles* in Limington, Maine. While waiting for ski season, Mark helps Guy with his apple orchard where he serves donuts and drives a small train offering rides to visiting children. There's more . . . but you'll have to reach the end of his chapter!

The family room opens to the working kitchen and is often the 'go to' room. Mark painted the walls with Old Village 'Rittenhouse Ivory' and the trim with 'Salem Brick'. Mark enjoys collecting early quilts and repurposed a goat cart into a table showcasing a few of his quilts.

Mark purchased the blue checked couch at Country Treasures in Shapleigh, Maine. The Chippendale couch alongside was a 'side of the road' find that Mark covered with a slipcover to conceal its unacceptable fabric.

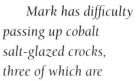

The tall clock is one of many clocks that Mark owns. This one was found in a farmhouse in Caribou, Maine, and while not the most valuable in his collection, its chime is lovely.

Mark has difficulty passing up cobalt salt-glazed crocks, three of which are displayed beneath the splay-legged bench. The bench demonstrates the lengths that many of us will go to get our hands on a treasured piece. Mark found the bench at a transfer station and had to dive into the dumpster to pull it out, much to the chagrin of a guard who continued to shout at Mark until he left the premises.

Mark enjoys early advertising containers with two caveats; they have to be colorful and they have to be priced at less than $1.00.

The pine chest shown left holds a 4' tall feather tree filled with old Christopher Radko Santa ornaments. Displayed around the base are some of Mark's Santa collections by other artists.

Tom Penney of Country Treasures in Shapleigh built the large cupboard that conceals the refrigerator. He also installed the pine plank countertops.

Mark found the collection of small bottles at The Christmas Tree Shop and purchased the entire set. Each bottle features an antique postcard label, another of Mark's interests.

Two Blue Willow platters provide a nice contrast to the red paint and yellowware bowls: one blue banded and another decorated with seaweed.

Mark designed and Tom Penney built the green dry sink. More wonderful salt-glazed crocks stand on top beside a yellowware milk bowl.

Mark uses all of the Flow Blue and Blue Willow dinnerware on a daily basis. While he enjoys displaying the pieces where he can enjoy them, he's practical minded and admits they're 'not just for show'. The large lidded redware bowl on the top shelf was purchased at Primitives in Pine in Hollis, Maine.

Tom Penney made the shutters for each of the windows in the den. Mark chose Old Village 'Valley Forge Mustard' paint. Mark closes the shutters during intense sunshine to protect his fabrics and quilts.

The wall shelf holds a small fabric cow pull toy and a very old mantel clock with a light chime.

Mark used an antique seed packet rack to display his collection of antique Christmas postcards which he finds is a very affordable collectible; he locates most for $1.00. He also tucks a few postcards in the branches of the tree to tie it all together.

Mark purchased the pine jelly cupboard as an unfinished piece and finished it himself. The two gingerbread clocks on top are part of a collection numbering over a dozen. Originally the 19thC clocks were used as kitchen clocks and treasured for their elaborate cutouts. Mark kept them all wound until his children complained that all the chimes were driving them crazy!

Mark found the settle bench in an old inn in Massachusetts and knows that underneath it retains its original oxblood paint; he is anxious to scrape it down as soon as his schedule permits. In the meantime, it's the perfect spot for draping a very old colorful quilt.

Mark uses utility boxes around the house and fills them with smalls or vintage mason jars that are repurposed into candleholders.

When not collecting, teaching, writing, skiing, and working at the Paulin's apple orchard or *Country Collectibles*, Mark is making and selling traditional pies from his Maine state-licensed kitchen. In fact, he recently won First Prize in a baking contest besting over 100 other competitors. This is clearly a man of many interests!!

Chapter 13

^ ⚹ ^

Fred and Gail Gersch

When Fred and Gail Gersch discovered country antiques 50 years ago while on their honeymoon, they immediately began attending flea markets and auctions looking for pieces to begin homemaking. Neither Gail, who hails from New Jersey, or Fred, a native Texan, grew up with antiques; Fred shared his sainted mother's traditional, modern style. "When she visited our home she expressed her concern that she has to 'pinch her bottom on my son's chairs'".

Now a retired Lutheran pastor, Fred met Gail while interning in New Jersey and was assigned to many parishes that resulted in numerous moves over 35 years. Retiring in 2001, Fred and Gail chose to build their home in Midlothian, Texas to be close to children and grandchildren. Their home was built in 2012 with a 'New England vision' that reveals itself the minute a visitor enters the front door!

Gail admits that Fred is a bit more knowledgeable about antiques than she and more of a perfectionist as to the placement and display of their pieces. Gail knows the moment she walks in the house and sees the grin on Fred's face that indeed some piece or even a room has been rearranged in her absence.

Fred and Gail rely on their trips to New England to satisfy their antiquing needs. They now plan a month in Maine and travel freely up and down the coast, wandering west into New Hampshire and Vermont often without concern as to how to get their finds back to Texas. Readers soon notice that the dilemma hasn't slowed them down or hampered their vision!

The exterior paint is a Sherwin-Williams selection 'Resort Tan'. The plank door is 'Fiery Brown' also by Sherwin-Williams.

The walls throughout the house are painted 'Dover White' from Sherwin-Williams. Fred and Gail selected Sherwin-Williams 'Meadow Lark' for the trim in each room, and Gail used this color as a background on the floor she stenciled in the entrance.

Fred and Gail knew exactly how they wanted the floors to blend with the décor but found pine plank out of their budget and tile, common in Texas homes, unacceptable for the look they hoped to achieve. One day while waiting in their doctor's office, they looked down to discover exactly what they wanted. Gail went so far as to get down on her hands and knees to feel the floor's surface comprised of 4'X 8" wide vinyl planks. The look couldn't be more right for them.

The drop leaf table is a recent acquisition that Fred and Gail found buried under china platters in a shop in Wells, Maine. The Nativity on top consists of animals collected over the years, including a Maine lobster and, of course, a Texas longhorn! Fred found the flax wheel at a local garage sale and was thrilled with the $50 price tag as well as its hammered iron that verifies its age. The early tavern table in front of the sofa was purchased many years ago from Dave Procter Antiques at the New Hampshire Antique Dealers Show in Deerfield, New Hampshire.

The large artificial tree, shown above right, is decorated with a variety of dried fruits – oranges, grapefruit, apples, and limes, all of which Gail preserves in the freezer between seasons.

The beautiful corner cupboard is treasured because Fred's dad was a master craftsman and built it. Fred and Gail were in an antique shop one day and found a corner cupboard they loved but it was out of their price range. Fred took some measurements and was able to come home and draw the design for his father.

The Madame Alexander Cinderella doll was Gail's as a child; she sits beside a Teddy bear that belonged to their son as a child. The sheep pull toy is an antique. Pictured in the background is a wagon that Fred's dad built.

Fred and Gail eat dinner every night by candlelight at the circa 1700s New Hampshire farm table with original blue paint.

Fred built the shelf above the doorway using a pattern he saw years ago in Country Home Magazine. It's a popular design that Fred has willingly shared with their

fellow country decorators. One of the early buckets that Fred enjoys collecting is displayed on the shelf, much to the chagrin of Fred and Gail's children, who love to visit but cannot understand why they like 'all this old stuff'!

Many years ago, Gail copied the concept of festoon window treatments described in an Early American Life Magazine article. Gail used linen for all the curtains, then used the 'festoon' method of hanging them on a cord. The Santa figure is a reproduction. The crafted saltbox house was made by a parishioner who knew Fred's favorite style of home.

Gail and Fred purchased the open cupboard from an antique dealer in Texas. The cupboard retains

a great deal of its original dry green paint and dates to the mid-19thC; it is purportedly of Georgia origin. The shelves are filled with pewter – both old and new, as well as many redware pieces. Rather than simply appreciate their beauty, Fred and Gail use the new pewter and redware.

Found in Milford, New Hampshire on one of their annual antique trips, the cloth doll appears to be crafted with early fabric.

The early portrait is unsigned and was found at Round Top; Fred fondly refers to the sitter as 'Hannah'. The small corner cupboard is an early piece found in Orange, Massachusetts.

Gail and Fred use an early primitive box to showcase a small Nativity. The barn lantern alongside is an early piece.

The trencher at center table is filled with fresh fruit and nuts. The wedding band hogscrapers on either side are reproductions.

Edyth O'Neill from Fredericksburg, Texas is familiar to many of us for the hooked rug patterns she creates. Unbeknownst to me, she also paints and created the oil portrait between the windows. It hangs above a two-drawer blanket chest of New England origin. The penny rug on top is new.

Isn't the fireplace wall spectacular? Fred worked closely with the mason as he was unfamiliar with the colonial style that included a representative bake oven and tinderbox. When Fred and Gail sold their previous home, the new owners didn't want the wall and agreed to let Fred and Gail take it with them. The door to the right hides a television. The small cupboard on the left above the mantel is called a parson's cupboard that traditionally kept a bottle of spirits, a Bible, and a pewter plate ready for a home visit by the local parson. The early door of the cupboard was given to Fred and Gail by collector friend, Jean St. Clair. On the hearth, a hornbeam holds a treen spatula.

The blue dry sink left of the fireplace is moved often so that its original paint can be appreciated in numerous spots throughout the house. Fred loves treen and uses the nook beside the fireplace to display many treen measures, bowls, and pantry boxes.

The large barn lantern in the forefront holds a hand-poured flameless taper from Marsh Homestead Antiques. The lantern on the left end of the mantel is early as is the lantern hanging on the right, referred to by some as a baker's lantern.

Fred spent 12 years working at Log Cabin Village in Fort Worth, Texas where he conducted demonstrations of hearthside cooking using pioneer implements. He and Gail still occasionally use their fireplace for the same purpose and have used their tin kitchen to occasionally cook a Thanksgiving Day turkey.

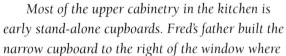

Most of the upper cabinetry in the kitchen is early stand-alone cupboards. Fred's father built the narrow cupboard to the right of the window where Gail stores her spices. The countertops are Formica which Gail chooses to age by covering them with early cutting boards.

Gail's father used the butcher block table in his butcher shop that once belonged to her grandfather. On the opposite wall, a graduated stack of four measures rests on top of a pine jelly cupboard dating to the 1800s. The redware plate is old.

Fred's dad made the large blue stepback that holds a nice collection of redware dishes; most were purchased at Old Sturbridge Village. The bottom shelf displays a village of saltbox houses and a Connecticut church from the former Lang and Wise Company.

Fred and Gail purchased the 19thC cupboard pictured above from Texas antique dealer Karen Buckingham. The piece, possibly from New Hampshire, retains remnants of original blue/gray paint and displays a warm worn patina.

The iron tripod rush light on the two-board top chair table from New England dates to the 1700s and was found at Brimfield, Massachusetts.

A newly-crafted doll found at Round Top sits in an early child's chair purchased at an estate sale. Fred was attracted to the chair due to its many early tin repairs.

Fred and Gail repurposed the laundry area to replicate an early buttery. An old door covers the top of the washer and dryer. The small space is filled with treen collectibles and smaller early cupboards; the blue hanging cupboard is Gail's favorite.

Gail stitched the framed Nativity sampler on the door.

Gail enjoys gardening and her herb garden in particular. Hanging on a stick in front of the window in the buttery is a cluster of flax. In front of the window are small pieces of yellow squash which Gail has suspended with a linen thread. During a museum visit, Gail witnessed how the colonists dried summer squash and then hydrated it for later use in soups.

Gail hand stitched all the bed linens on the master bedroom four-poster bed. It was a project she saved until she was fully retired and had the time and patience necessary to complete the task. The coverlet was found in Old Williamsburg, Virginia and resembles an authentic Linsey-Woolsey.

The peg rack between the windows holds an assortment of vintage aprons, a bonnet, and a shirt Fred wears when doing hearthside demonstrations at the Log Cabin Village. Fred made all the window shutters while his dad made the Shaker style hanging cupboard to the left of the bed.

A large vintage hatbox rests on the blanket chest at the foot of the bed. The chest was purchased from Karen Buckingham and retains original dry salmon paint.

On top of the bedside table, shown above right, a curtained box conceals a telephone and alarm clock!

The hanging cupboard purchased at Round Top boasts an early tombstone door with dry white paint. The table below was found in Comfort, Texas.

Fred and Gail found the slant top desk at Curry Antiques in Lancaster, Ohio. It's a bit more primitive than most of their pieces but its size and the corner space made it ideal. The appliquéd angel quilt above was made by Gail's friends as a gift. An iron silhouette of a child with candle can be seen in the window behind. A pattern for the window silhouette is shown on page 136.

The two-drawer pine chest was found at Round Top. It retains remnants of salmon paint and surprisingly conceals five drawers behind the doors, making it a perfect bureau for Gail.

Fred found the quilt on the guestroom bed in Nebraska and presented it to Gail as a Christmas present. The coverlet beneath is from Family Heirloom Weavers.

At the foot of the bed, a Connecticut blanket chest, one of Fred and Gail's favorite antiques, stands beside a ratchet candlestand made by Fred's father.

Fred and Gail use the third bedroom as a parlor. The mantel came out of a 19thC Cape Cod home. The portrait over the mantel was a Round Top find, while the hooked rug on the hearth is a new piece. The door to the right of the mantel was salvaged from Fred's grandmother's farm.

The loveseat was found at an antique mall in Texas and reupholstered with fabric that Fred and Gail purchased from The Angel House in Brookfield, Massachusetts.

Fred's dad built the Shaker style case in front which holds a rare German Bible that once belonged to Fred's great-grandfather. The Bible dates to 1792.

Collections of early leather bound books and small boxes are displayed on a cant back wall shelf purchased at Doty Antiques. In the lower right corner, a miniature house reminds Fred of his grandparent's farmhouse depicted in the background photograph.

Fred searched long and hard for an affordable feather tree and was delighted to find the 4' tree marked 50% off during a post-holiday sale. Jack O'Neill made the surround fence.

Fred and Gail enjoy being at home near family but are nowhere near ready to give up their annual antiquing trips. Fred said, "As long as I can go to New England once a year for my New England fix, I'm good!"

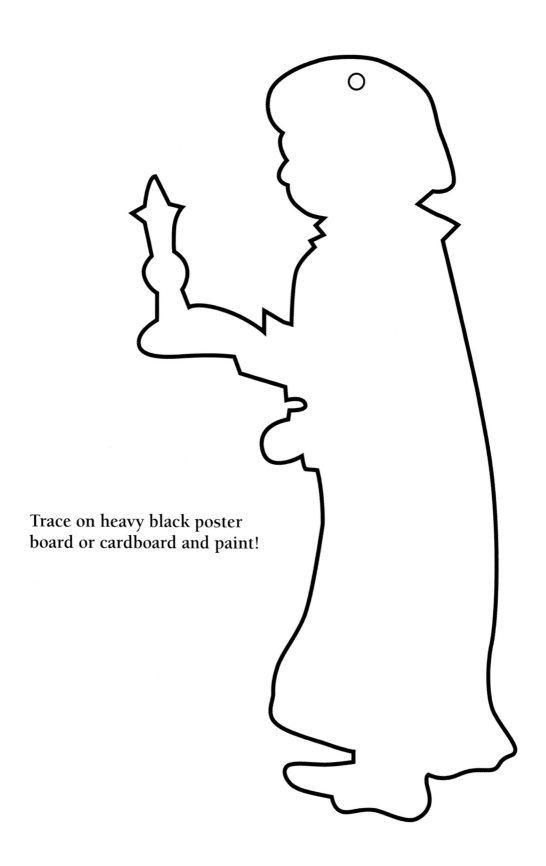

Trace on heavy black poster
board or cardboard and paint!

Chapter 14

Mike and Lori Corelis

Michael and Lori Ann Corelis of Westerville, Ohio are no strangers to the 'simply country' book series as they were kind enough to share their experience with building a kitchen garden or potager in my previous book, *Along the Garden Path*. And last year they gave us a sneak preview into their holiday decorated home in *A Country Christmas*.

Lori Ann and Michael met and married 14 years ago, blending and raising three children in a new home (Michael's preference) but decorated in a country style (Lori Ann's preference). The result is striking!

Lori Ann is always creating something, whether it be in the garden or something from her sewing room. As the daughter of a seamstress, she is blessed with the sewing gene and passion for textiles. The reader will see them tastefully displayed in many rooms. Lori Ann sells her pieces on her website *www.thespottedhare.com* and also at a few shows each year. Lori Ann also maintains a blog *Lorianncorelis.blogspot.com*.

Sitting on the back deck, a concrete tombstone angel with ice covering half its face offers an interesting effect.

The antique quilt above the fireplace is rendered in a pattern called 'A Fan'. The composition is a variety of fabrics and wools chosen for the richness of their colors. It has a number of embroidered signatures indicating it may have been created by a church or ladies group.

Lori Ann decorated the mantel in a woodland theme using greens and pinecones. A group of ugly jugs, one of Lori Ann's favorite collections, nestles amidst the greenery. The collection is the work of many artists, two of whom are Jim McDowell and Grace Hewell. The Woodland Santa figure was crafted by artist Scott Smith of rucusstudio.com.

The 19thC pine blanket chest retains remnants of red wash. Lori appreciates the simplicity of the piece.

Lori Ann dressed a vintage child's mannequin on the hearth in an early child's vest and top hat.

In A Country Christmas, Lori Ann shared her recipe for making dried citrus ornaments that she uses abundantly throughout the house for the aroma they provide during the season.

The Ohio pie safe, purchased in Lebanon, Ohio, dates to the 19thC and retains its original oxblood red paint. A close-up picture shows the detail of the tins and the unique pattern of three columns with a bird on top.

Lori Ann has a collection of 'feet', displayed on top of the pie safe; the sign above appropriately reads 'Foot'.

In the two story living room, blanket chests reach up the wall and one of Lori Ann's Teddy bear creations sits in a make-do chair by Hoffman-Woodard of PA" (hoffmanwoodward.com). Lori Ann is drawn to original dry painted pieces and enjoys the graduated stack of chests that requires limited space but features an eye-appealing array of colors.

Lacy, their Australian sheepdog, adds her two cents worth at the end of the chapter with her willingness to share her recipe for holiday dog treats.

On the front entrance wall, Lori Ann displays a large, framed antique child's velvet quilt.

Isn't the surface of the 19thC New England red cupboard magnificent? Lori Ann purchased it years ago from a friend.

A 19thC large treen doughbowl holds boxwood and pine sprays that enclose a flameless pillar candle from Marsh Homestead Antiques.

Lori Ann describes her kitchen as cozy with a view out the deck doors. The Viking range came with the home, but was something Lori Ann wanted for years as she previously owned a restaurant and catering business. She appreciates her collections of yellowware and stoneware crocks for their usefulness.

Sitting on top of the pine apothecary is an early basket which holds a unique 6" Steiff bear.

Next to the balcony overlooking the Great Room an antique basket sits on an early chair. Nestled into this basket is an early quilt remnant, a mohair bear that Lori Ann made and an antique velvet star which could have been a small pillow or a pincushion.

The cats atop the lovely 19thC putty-colored jelly cupboard date also to the same period. They are made with printed fabric produced by Arnold Print Works in North Adams, Massachusetts.

The coverlet at the foot of the master bedroom bed is from Family Heirloom Weavers.

Lori Ann uses the glass front cupboard to store and showcase a collection of vintage quilts, Family Heirloom pieces, and remnants of early coverlets.

Another of Scott Smith's Santa figures stands on top of an early pine chest with clean, simple lines. The chest dates to the 19thC and retains its red wash.

Lori Ann is drawn to textiles, as the peg rack holds an antique child's jacket, hats, and mittens, as well as a vintage top hat and Family Heirloom Weaver throw.

Sitting on the guestroom bed is a doll made by folk artist Nicole Sayer (nicolsayer.com). Beside the doll are two antique dolls – one with a porcelain head and the second with a paper mache head.

The blue dress pictured below right was worn by Lori Ann's mother as a child.

I love the way Lori Ann displays a unique collection of children's shoes! Because she does a number of shows each year, she often chooses antique smalls from her house to use as props for her booth. That means she gets to enjoy them and the rationale makes it easy to justify the purchase as they are needed for her work!

A simple child's red wool dress is not only perfect for holiday season but Lori Ann's favorite color.

Lori Ann and Michael use one of their rooms as an office. An early tavern table with red wash base and breadboard ends scrub top holds a Coates vintage sewing cabinet. Hanging above is an antique child's quilt.

Resting against a salt-glazed cobalt decorated stoneware crock, an early Steiff bear looks as though he's content to stay there for a while.

Lori Ann is drawn to early toys, particularly those on metal wheels. Three Steiff pull toys that predate the well-known Steiff bears are pictured on the middle shelf – an elephant, a dog, and a sheep.

An early cheese basket holds three more vintage Steiff bears with a flameless candle.

Lori Ann's sewing room is a workroom that she prefers to keep more "pretty" for the inspiration. She often chooses "pretty" over "practical" but manages to make it work!

The table holds an array of working projects and a yellow and red pin cushion crafted by Hoffman and Woodward. *Heidi Howard painted the sign above that identifies Lori Ann's business,* The Spotted Hare. *Hanging above is an enormous pair of tailor scissors.*

Lori Ann's business and now teaching needlework as well takes up most of her creative time, however in a rare stolen moment she also enjoys rug hooking and wool appliqué. She can't envision ever sitting idle as it just isn't in her nature.

Lori Ann and Michael's priorities recently have centered around family some health concerns and caregiving Lori Ann's elderly mother. Lori Ann has been off the antique trail for a little while but she looks forward to continuing the hunt in time, despite her comment, "We're full up."

Lori Ann loves the inspiration she receives from visiting shows and antique shops and finds herself oftentimes rejuvenated simply by the colors she encounters. Because she has always bought what she loves, Lori Ann feels no urgency to sell and replace or upgrade. In addition, the fact that Lori Ann likes

a little bit of everything occasionally creates a dilemma.

I can't imagine that this talented woman needs inspiration as she never seems short of a new clever idea, a craft to showcase, or a decorating talent to share with all of us – for which I'm thankful!

How to Make Dog Treats

Ingredients:

2 cups whole wheat flour

1 cup yellow cornmeal

1/2 teaspoon garlic powder

1 large egg

1 tablespoon olive oil

1 cup chicken, beef, or vegetable broth

Directions:

- Mix the dry ingredients. Beat egg, oil, and broth, then add to the dry mixture.

- Roll out to a scant 1/4" thickness using a bit more cornmeal to prevent sticking to the surface.

- Cut with your favorite cookie cutters.

- Bake on an ungreased cookie sheet at 325° F, turning halfway thru the baking.

- Bake 25-35 minutes until the dough is dry and hard like a cracker. Let sit overnight to dry completely before packaging. The recipe is easily doubled or even tripled if you have lots of doggie friends!